DOCTOR FAUSTUS: TEXT B

CHRISTOPHER MARLOWE

ISBN: 978-1503019805

DRAMATIS PERSONAE:

THE POPE.
THE EMPEROR OF GERMANY.
RAYMOND, king of Hungary.
DUKE OF SAXONY.
BRUNO.
DUKE OF VANHOLT.
MARTINO, |
FREDERICK, | gentlemen.
BENVOLIO, |
FAUSTUS.
VALDES, | friends to FAUSTUS.
CORNELIUS, |
WAGNER, servant to FAUSTUS.
Clown.
ROBIN.
DICK.
Vintner.
Horse-courser.
Carter.
An Old Man.
Scholars, Cardinals, ARCHBISHOP OF RHEIMS, Bishops, Monks,
    Friars, Soldiers, and Attendants.

DUCHESS OF VANHOLT.
Hostess.

LUCIFER.
BELZEBUB.
MEPHISTOPHILIS.
Good Angel.
Evil Angel.
The Seven Deadly Sins.
Devils.
Spirits in the shapes of ALEXANDER THE GREAT, of his Paramour,
of DARIUS, and of HELEN.

THE TRAGICAL HISTORY OF DOCTOR FAUSTUS
FROM THE QUARTO OF 1616

Enter CHORUS.

CHORUS. Not marching in the fields of Thrasymene,
Where Mars did mate the warlike Carthagens;
Nor sporting in the dalliance of love,
In courts of kings where state is overturn'd;
Nor in the pomp of proud audacious deeds,
Intends our Muse to vaunt her heavenly verse:
Only this, gentles,—we must now perform
The form of Faustus' fortunes, good or bad:
And now to patient judgments we appeal,
And speak for Faustus in his infancy.
Now is he born of parents base of stock,
In Germany, within a town call'd Rhodes:
At riper years, to Wittenberg he went,
Whereas his kinsmen chiefly brought him up.
So much he profits in divinity,
That shortly he was grac'd with doctor's name,
Excelling all, and sweetly can dispute
In th' heavenly matters of theology;
Till swoln with cunning, of a self-conceit,
His waxen wings did mount above his reach,
And, melting, heavens conspir'd his overthrow;
For, falling to a devilish exercise,
And glutted now with learning's golden gifts,
He surfeits upon cursed necromancy;
Nothing so sweet as magic is to him,
Which he prefers before his chiefest bliss:
And this the man that in his study sits.
    [Exit.]

FAUSTUS discovered in his study.

FAUSTUS. Settle thy studies, Faustus, and begin
To sound the depth of that thou wilt profess:
Having commenc'd, be a divine in show,
Yet level at the end of every art,
And live and die in Aristotle's works.
Sweet Analytics, 'tis thou hast ravish'd me!
Bene disserere est finis logices.

Is, to dispute well, logic's chiefest end?
Affords this art no greater miracle?
Then read no more; thou hast attain'd that end:
A greater subject fitteth Faustus' wit:
Bid Economy farewell, and Galen come:
Be a physician, Faustus; heap up gold,
And be eterniz'd for some wondrous cure:
Summum bonum medicinoe sanitas,
The end of physic is our body's health.
Why, Faustus, hast thou not attain'd that end?
Are not thy bills hung up as monuments,
Whereby whole cities have escap'd the plague,
And thousand desperate maladies been cur'd?
Yet art thou still but Faustus, and a man.
Couldst thou make men to live eternally,
Or, being dead, raise them to life again,
Then this profession were to be esteem'd.
Physic, farewell! Where is Justinian?

    [Reads.]
Si una eademque res legatur duobus, alter rem,
alter valorem rei, &c.

A petty case of paltry legacies!

    [Reads.]
Exhoereditare filium non potest pater, nisi, &c.

Such is the subject of the institute,
And universal body of the law:
This study fits a mercenary drudge,
Who aims at nothing but external trash;
Too servile and illiberal for me.
When all is done, divinity is best:
Jerome's Bible, Faustus; view it well.

    [Reads.]
Stipendium peccati mors est.
              Ha!
                    Stipendium, &c.

The reward of sin is death: that's hard.

[Reads.]
Si peccasse negamus, fallimur, et nulla est in nobis veritas;

If we say that we have no sin, we deceive ourselves, and there
is no truth in us. Why, then, belike we must sin, and so
consequently die:
Ay, we must die an everlasting death.
What doctrine call you this, Che sera, sera,
What will be, shall be? Divinity, adieu!

These metaphysics of magicians,
And necromantic books are heavenly;
Lines, circles, scenes, letters, and characters;
Ay, these are those that Faustus most desires.
O, what a world of profit and delight,
Of power, of honour, and omnipotence,
Is promis'd to the studious artizan!
All things that move between the quiet poles
Shall be at my command: emperors and kings

Are but obeyed in their several provinces;
But his dominion that exceeds in this,
Stretcheth as far as doth the mind of man;
A sound magician is a demigod:
Here tire, my brains, to gain a deity.

        Enter WAGNER.

Wagner, commend me to my dearest friends,
The German Valdes and Cornelius;
Request them earnestly to visit me.

WAGNER. I will, sir.
    [Exit.]

FAUSTUS. Their conference will be a greater help to me
Than all my labours, plod I ne'er so fast.

        Enter GOOD ANGEL and EVIL ANGEL.

GOOD ANGEL. O, Faustus, lay that damned book aside,
And gaze not on it, lest it tempt thy soul,
And heap God's heavy wrath upon thy head!
Read, read the Scriptures:—that is blasphemy.

EVIL ANGEL. Go forward, Faustus, in that famous art
Wherein all Nature's treasure is contain'd:
Be thou on earth as Jove is in the sky,
Lord and commander of these elements.
    [Exeunt ANGELS.]

FAUSTUS. How am I glutted with conceit of this!
Shall I make spirits fetch me what I please,
Resolve me of all ambiguities,
Perform what desperate enterprise I will?
I'll have them fly to India for gold,
Ransack the ocean for orient pearl,
And search all corners of the new-found world
For pleasant fruits and princely delicates;
I'll have them read me strange philosophy,
And tell the secrets of all foreign kings;
I'll have them wall all Germany with brass,
And make swift Rhine circle fair Wertenberg;
I'll have them fill the public schools with silk,
Wherewith the students shall be bravely clad;
I'll levy soldiers with the coin they bring,
And chase the Prince of Parma from our land,
And reign sole king of all the provinces;
Yea, stranger engines for the brunt of war,
Than was the fiery keel at Antwerp-bridge,
I'll make my servile spirits to invent.

    Enter VALDES and CORNELIUS.

Come, German Valdes, and Cornelius,
And make me blest with your sage conference.
Valdes, sweet Valdes, and Cornelius,
Know that your words have won me at the last
To practice magic and concealed arts.
Philosophy is odious and obscure;
Both law and physic are for petty wits:
'Tis magic, magic that hath ravish'd me.
Then, gentle friends, aid me in this attempt;
And I, that have with subtle syllogisms
Gravell'd the pastors of the German church,
And made the flowering pride of Wittenberg
Swarm to my problems, as th' infernal spirits
On sweet Musaeus when he came to hell,

Will be as cunning as Agrippa was,
Whose shadow made all Europe honour him.

VALDES. Faustus, these books, thy wit, and our experience,
Shall make all nations to canonize us.
As Indian Moors obey their Spanish lords,
So shall the spirits of every element
Be always serviceable to us three;
Like lions shall they guard us when we please;
Like Almain rutters with their horsemen's staves,
Or Lapland giants, trotting by our sides;
Sometimes like women, or unwedded maids,
Shadowing more beauty in their airy brows
Than have the white breasts of the queen of love:
From Venice shall they drag huge argosies,
And from America the golden fleece
That yearly stuffs old Philip's treasury;
If learned Faustus will be resolute.

FAUSTUS. Valdes, as resolute am I in this
As thou to live: therefore object it not.

CORNELIUS. The miracles that magic will perform
Will make thee vow to study nothing else.
He that is grounded in astrology,
Enrich'd with tongues, well seen in minerals,
Hath all the principles magic doth require:
Then doubt not, Faustus, but to be renowm'd,
And more frequented for this mystery
Than heretofore the Delphian oracle.
The spirits tell me they can dry the sea,
And fetch the treasure of all foreign wrecks,
Yea, all the wealth that our forefathers hid
Within the massy entrails of the earth:
Then tell me, Faustus, what shall we three want?

FAUSTUS. Nothing, Cornelius. O, this cheers my soul!
Come, shew me some demonstrations magical,
That I may conjure in some bushy grove,
And have these joys in full possession.

VALDES. Then haste thee to some solitary grove,
And bear wise Bacon's and Albertus' works,

The Hebrew Psalter, and New Testament;
And whatsoever else is requisite
We will inform thee ere our conference cease.

CORNELIUS. Valdes, first let him know the words of art;
And then, all other ceremonies learn'd,
Faustus may try his cunning by himself.

VALDES. First I'll instruct thee in the rudiments,
And then wilt thou be perfecter than I.

FAUSTUS. Then come and dine with me, and, after meat,
We'll canvass every quiddity thereof;
For, ere I sleep, I'll try what I can do:
This night I'll conjure, though I die therefore.
   [Exeunt.]

   Enter two SCHOLARS.

FIRST SCHOLAR. I wonder what's become of Faustus, that was wont to make our schools ring with sic probo.

SECOND SCHOLAR. That shall we presently know; here comes his boy.

   Enter WAGNER.

FIRST SCHOLAR. How now, sirrah! where's thy master?

WAGNER. God in heaven knows.

SECOND SCHOLAR. Why, dost not thou know, then?

WAGNER. Yes, I know; but that follows not.

FIRST SCHOLAR. Go to, sirrah! leave your jesting, and tell us where he is.

WAGNER. That follows not by force of argument, which you, being licentiates, should stand upon: therefore acknowledge your error, and be attentive.

SECOND SCHOLAR. Then you will not tell us?

WAGNER. You are deceived, for I will tell you: yet, if you were not dunces, you would never ask me such a question; for is he not corpus naturale? and is not that mobile? then wherefore should you ask me such a question? But that I am by nature phlegmatic, slow to wrath, and prone to lechery (to love, I would say), it were not for you to come within forty foot of the place of execution, although I do not doubt but to see you both hanged the next sessions. Thus having triumphed over you, I will set my countenance like a precisian, and begin to speak thus:—Truly, my dear brethren, my master is within at dinner, with Valdes and Cornelius, as this wine, if it could speak, would inform your worships: and so, the Lord bless you, preserve you, and keep you, my dear brethren!
    [Exit.]

FIRST SCHOLAR. O Faustus!
Then I fear that which I have long suspected,
That thou art fall'n into that damned art
For which they two are infamous through the world.

SECOND SCHOLAR. Were he a stranger, not allied to me,
The danger of his soul would make me mourn.
But, come, let us go and inform the Rector:
It may be his grave counsel may reclaim him.

FIRST SCHOLAR. I fear me nothing will reclaim him now.

SECOND SCHOLAR. Yet let us see what we can do.
    [Exeunt.]

    Enter FAUSTUS.

FAUSTUS. Now that the gloomy shadow of the night,
Longing to view Orion's drizzling look,
Leaps from th' antartic world unto the sky,
And dims the welkin with her pitchy breath,
Faustus, begin thine incantations,
And try if devils will obey thy hest,
Seeing thou hast pray'd and sacrific'd to them.
Within this circle is Jehovah's name,
Forward and backward anagrammatiz'd,
Th' abbreviated names of holy saints,
Figures of every adjunct to the heavens,

And characters of signs and erring stars,
By which the spirits are enforc'd to rise:
Then fear not, Faustus, to be resolute,
And try the utmost magic can perform.
   [Thunder.]
Sint mihi dii Acherontis propitii! Valeat numen triplex Jehovoe!
Ignei, aerii, aquatani spiritus, salvete! Orientis princeps
Belzebub, inferni ardentis monarcha, et Demogorgon, propitiamus
vos, ut appareat et surgat Mephistophilis Dragon, quod tumeraris:
per Jehovam, Gehennam, et consecratam aquam quam nunc spargo,
signumque crucis quod nunc facio, et per vota nostra, ipse nunc
surgat nobis dicatus Mephistophilis!

   Enter MEPHISTOPHILIS.

I charge thee to return, and change thy shape;
Thou art too ugly to attend on me:
Go, and return an old Franciscan friar;
That holy shape becomes a devil best.
   [Exit MEPHISTOPHILIS.]

I see there's virtue in my heavenly words.
Who would not be proficient in this art?
How pliant is this Mephistophilis,
Full of obedience and humility!
Such is the force of magic and my spells.

   Re-enter MEPHISTOPHILIS like a Franciscan friar.

MEPHIST. Now, Faustus, what wouldst thou have me do?

FAUSTUS. I charge thee wait upon me whilst I live,
To do whatever Faustus shall command,
Be it to make the moon drop from her sphere,
Or the ocean to overwhelm the world.

MEPHIST. I am a servant to great Lucifer,
And may not follow thee without his leave:
No more than he commands must we perform.

FAUSTUS. Did not he charge thee to appear to me?

MEPHIST. No, I came hither of mine own accord.

FAUSTUS. Did not my conjuring speeches raise thee? speak!

MEPHIST. That was the cause, but yet per accidens;
For, when we hear one rack the name of God,
Abjure the Scriptures and his Saviour Christ,
We fly, in hope to get his glorious soul;
Nor will we come, unless he use such means
Whereby he is in danger to be damn'd.
Therefore the shortest cut for conjuring
Is stoutly to abjure all godliness,
And pray devoutly to the prince of hell.

FAUSTUS. So Faustus hath
Already done; and holds this principle,
There is no chief but only Belzebub;
To whom Faustus doth dedicate himself.
This word "damnation" terrifies not me,
For I confound hell in Elysium:
My ghost be with the old philosophers!
But, leaving these vain trifles of men's souls,
Tell me what is that Lucifer thy lord?

MEPHIST. Arch-regent and commander of all spirits.

FAUSTUS. Was not that Lucifer an angel once?

MEPHIST. Yes, Faustus, and most dearly lov'd of God.

FAUSTUS. How comes it, then, that he is prince of devils?

MEPHIST. O, by aspiring pride and insolence;
For which God threw him from the face of heaven.

FAUSTUS. And what are you that live with Lucifer?

MEPHIST. Unhappy spirits that fell with Lucifer,
Conspir'd against our God with Lucifer,
And are for ever damn'd with Lucifer.

FAUSTUS. Where are you damn'd?

MEPHIST. In hell.

FAUSTUS. How comes it, then, that thou art out of hell?

MEPHIST. Why, this is hell, nor am I out of it:
Think'st thou that I, that saw the face of God,
And tasted the eternal joys of heaven,
Am not tormented with ten thousand hells,
In being depriv'd of everlasting bliss?
O, Faustus, leave these frivolous demands,
Which strike a terror to my fainting soul!

FAUSTUS. What, is great Mephistophilis so passionate
For being deprived of the joys of heaven?
Learn thou of Faustus manly fortitude,
And scorn those joys thou never shalt possess.
Go bear these tidings to great Lucifer:
Seeing Faustus hath incurr'd eternal death
By desperate thoughts against Jove's deity,
Say, he surrenders up to him his soul,
So he will spare him four and twenty years,
Letting him live in all voluptuousness;
Having thee ever to attend on me,
To give me whatsoever I shall ask,
To tell me whatsoever I demand,
To slay mine enemies, and to aid my friends,
And always be obedient to my will.
Go, and return to mighty Lucifer,
And meet me in my study at midnight,
And then resolve me of thy master's mind.

MEPHIST. I will, Faustus.
    [Exit.]

FAUSTUS. Had I as many souls as there be stars,
I'd give them all for Mephistophilis.
By him I'll be great emperor of the world,
And make a bridge thorough the moving air,
To pass the ocean with a band of men;
I'll join the hills that bind the Afric shore,
And make that country continent to Spain,
And both contributary to my crown:
The Emperor shall not live but by my leave,
Nor any potentate of Germany.

Now that I have obtain'd what I desir'd,
I'll live in speculation of this art,
Till Mephistophilis return again.
    [Exit.]

    Enter WAGNER and CLOWN.

WAGNER. Come hither, sirrah boy.

CLOWN. Boy! O, disgrace to my person! zounds, boy in your face!
You have seen many boys with beards, I am sure.

WAGNER. Sirrah, hast thou no comings in?

CLOWN. Yes, and goings out too, you may see, sir.

WAGNER. Alas, poor slave! see how poverty jests in his nakedness! I
know the villain's out of service, and so hungry, that I know he would give
his soul to the devil for a shoulder of mutton,
though it were blood-raw.

CLOWN. Not so neither: I had need to have it well roasted, and
good sauce to it, if I pay so dear, I can tell you.

WAGNER. Sirrah, wilt thou be my man, and wait on me, and I will
make thee go like Qui mihi discipulus?

CLOWN. What, in verse?

WAGNER. No, slave; in beaten silk and staves-acre.

CLOWN. Staves-acre! that's good to kill vermin: then, belike,
if I serve you, I shall be lousy.

WAGNER. Why, so thou shalt be, whether thou dost it or no; for,
sirrah, if thou dost not presently bind thyself to me for seven
years, I'll turn all the lice about thee into familiars, and make
them tear thee in pieces.

CLOWN. Nay, sir, you may save yourself a labour, for they
are as familiar with me as if they paid for their meat and drink,
I can tell you.

WAGNER. Well, sirrah, leave your jesting, and take these guilders.
[Gives money.]

CLOWN. Yes, marry, sir; and I thank you too.

WAGNER. So, now thou art to be at an hour's warning, whensoever and
wheresoever the devil shall fetch thee.

CLOWN. Here, take your guilders again; I'll none of 'em.

WAGNER. Not I; thou art pressed: prepare thyself, or I will
presently raise up two devils to carry thee away.—Banio! Belcher!

CLOWN. Belcher! an Belcher come here, I'll belch him: I am not
afraid of a devil.

    Enter two DEVILS.

WAGNER. How now, sir! will you serve me now?

CLOWN. Ay, good Wagner; take away the devils, then.

WAGNER. Spirits, away!
[Exeunt DEVILS.]
Now, sirrah, follow me.

CLOWN. I will, sir: but hark you, master; will you teach me this
conjuring occupation?

WAGNER. Ay, sirrah, I'll teach thee to turn thyself to a dog,
or a cat, or a mouse, or a rat, or any thing.

CLOWN. A dog, or a cat, or a mouse, or a rat!
O, brave, Wagner!

WAGNER. Villain, call me Master Wagner, and see that you walk
attentively, and let your right eye be always diametrally fixed
upon my left heel, that thou mayst quasi vestigiis nostris
insistere.

CLOWN. Well, sir, I warrant you.
[Exeunt.]

FAUSTUS discovered in his study.

FAUSTUS. Now, Faustus,
Must thou needs be damn'd, canst thou not be sav'd.
What boots it, then, to think on God or heaven?
Away with such vain fancies, and despair;
Despair in God, and trust in Belzebub:
Now, go not backward, Faustus; be resolute:
Why waver'st thou? O, something soundeth in mine ear,
"Abjure this magic, turn to God again!"
Why, he loves thee not;
The god thou serv'st is thine own appetite,
Wherein is fix'd the love of Belzebub:
To him I'll build an altar and a church,
And offer lukewarm blood of new-born babes.

Enter GOOD ANGEL and EVIL ANGEL.

EVIL ANGEL. Go forward, Faustus, in that famous art.

GOOD ANGEL. Sweet Faustus, leave that execrable art.

FAUSTUS. Contrition, prayer, repentance—what of these?

GOOD ANGEL. O, they are means to bring thee unto heaven!

EVIL ANGEL. Rather illusions, fruits of lunacy,
That make men foolish that do use them most.

GOOD ANGEL. Sweet Faustus, think of heaven and heavenly things.

EVIL ANGEL. No, Faustus; think of honour and of wealth.
   [Exeunt ANGELS.]

FAUSTUS. Wealth!
Why, the signiory of Embden shall be mine.
When Mephistophilis shall stand by me,
What power can hurt me? Faustus, thou art safe:
Cast no more doubts.—Mephistophilis, come,
And bring glad tidings from great Lucifer;—
Is't not midnight?—come Mephistophilis,
And bring glad tidings from great Lucifer;—
Is't not midnight?—come Mephistophilis,

Veni, veni, Mephistophile!

Enter MEPHISTOPHILIS.

Now tell me what saith Lucifer, thy lord?

MEPHIST. That I shall wait on Faustus whilst he lives,
So he will buy my service with his soul.

FAUSTUS. Already Faustus hath hazarded that for thee.

MEPHIST. But now thou must bequeath it solemnly,
And write a deed of gift with thine own blood;
For that security craves Lucifer.
If thou deny it, I must back to hell.

FAUSTUS. Stay, Mephistophilis, and tell me, what good will my
soul do thy lord?

MEPHIST. Enlarge his kingdom.

FAUSTUS. Is that the reason why he tempts us thus?

MEPHIST. Solamen miseris socios habuisse doloris.

FAUSTUS. Why, have you any pain that torture others?

MEPHIST. As great as have the human souls of men.
But, tell me, Faustus, shall I have thy soul?
And I will be thy slave, and wait on thee,
And give thee more than thou hast wit to ask.

FAUSTUS. Ay, Mephistophilis, I'll give it thee.

MEPHIST. Then, Faustus, stab thine arm courageously,
And bind thy soul, that at some certain day
Great Lucifer may claim it as his own;
And then be thou as great as Lucifer.

FAUSTUS. [Stabbing his arm] Lo, Mephistophilis, for love of thee,
Faustus hath cut his arm, and with his proper blood
Assures his soul to be great Lucifer's,
Chief lord and regent of perpetual night!

View here this blood that trickles from mine arm,
And let it be propitious for my wish.

MEPHIST. But, Faustus,
Write it in manner of a deed of gift.

FAUSTUS. [Writing] Ay, so I do. But, Mephistophilis,
My blood congeals, and I can write no more.

MEPHIST. I'll fetch thee fire to dissolve it straight.
    [Exit.]

FAUSTUS. What might the staying of my blood portend?
Is it unwilling I should write this bill?
Why streams it not, that I may write afresh?
FAUSTUS GIVES TO THEE HIS SOUL: O, there it stay'd!
Why shouldst thou not? is not thy soul thine own?
Then write again, FAUSTUS GIVES TO THEE HIS SOUL.

    Re-enter MEPHISTOPHILIS with the chafer of fire.

MEPHIST. See, Faustus, here is fire; set it on.

FAUSTUS. So, now the blood begins to clear again;
Now will I make an end immediately.
    [Writes.]

MEPHIST. What will not I do to obtain his soul?
    [Aside.]

FAUSTUS. Consummatum est; this bill is ended,
And Faustus hath bequeath'd his soul to Lucifer.
But what is this inscription on mine arm?
Homo, fuge: whither should I fly?
If unto God, he'll throw me down to hell.
My senses are deceiv'd; here's nothing writ:—
O, yes, I see it plain; even here is writ,
Homo, fuge: yet shall not Faustus fly.

MEPHIST. I'll fetch him somewhat to delight his mind.
    [Aside, and then exit.]

    Enter DEVILS, giving crowns and rich apparel to FAUSTUS.

They dance, and then depart.

Re-enter MEPHISTOPHILIS.

FAUSTUS. What means this show? speak, Mephistophilis.

MEPHIST. Nothing, Faustus, but to delight thy mind,
And let thee see what magic can perform.

FAUSTUS. But may I raise such spirits when I please?

MEPHIST. Ay, Faustus, and do greater things than these.

FAUSTUS. Then, Mephistophilis, receive this scroll,
A deed of gift of body and of soul:
But yet conditionally that thou perform
All covenants and articles between us both!

MEPHIST. Faustus, I swear by hell and Lucifer
To effect all promises between us both!

FAUSTUS. Then hear me read it, Mephistophilis.
    [Reads.]
ON THESE CONDITIONS FOLLOWING. FIRST, THAT FAUSTUS
MAY BE A SPIRIT IN FORM AND SUBSTANCE. SECONDLY, THAT
MEPHISTOPHILIS SHALL BE HIS SERVANT, AND BE BY HIM
COMMANDED. THIRDLY, THAT
    MEPHISTOPHILIS SHALL DO FOR HIM, AND BRING HIM
WHATSOEVER HE DESIRES. FOURTHLY, THAT HE SHALL BE IN
HIS CHAMBER OR HOUSE INVISIBLE. LASTLY, THAT HE SHALL
APPEAR TO THE SAID JOHN FAUSTUS,
    AT ALL TIMES, IN WHAT SHAPE AND FORM SOEVER HE
PLEASE. I, JOHN FAUSTUS, OF WITTENBERG, DOCTOR, BY
THESE PRESENTS, DO GIVE BOTH BODY AND SOUL TO
LUCIFER PRINCE OF THE EAST, AND HIS MINISTER
    MEPHISTOPHILIS; AND FURTHERMORE GRANT UNTO THEM,
THAT, FOUR-AND-TWENTY YEARS BEING EXPIRED, AND
THESE ARTICLES ABOVE-WRITTEN BEING INVIOLATE, FULL
POWER TO FETCH OR CARRY THE SAID JOHN FAUSTUS, BODY
AND SOUL, FLESH AND BLOOD, INTO THEIR HABITATION
WHERESOEVER. BY ME, JOHN FAUSTUS.

MEPHIST. Speak, Faustus, do you deliver this as your deed?

FAUSTUS. Ay, take it, and the devil give thee good of it!

MEPHIST. So, now, Faustus, ask me what thou wilt.

FAUSTUS. First I will question with thee about hell.
Tell me, where is the place that men call hell?

MEPHIST. Under the heavens.

FAUSTUS. Ay, so are all things else; but whereabouts?

MEPHIST. Within the bowels of these elements,
Where we are tortur'd and remain for ever:
Hell hath no limits, nor is circumscrib'd
In one self-place; but where we are is hell,
And where hell is, there must we ever be:
And, to be short, when all the world dissolves,
And every creature shall be purified,
All places shall be hell that are not heaven.

FAUSTUS. I think hell's a fable.

MEPHIST. Ay, think so still, till experience change thy mind.

FAUSTUS. Why, dost thou think that Faustus shall be damn'd?

MEPHIST. Ay, of necessity, for here's the scroll
In which thou hast given thy soul to Lucifer.

FAUSTUS. Ay, and body too; and what of that?
Think'st thou that Faustus is so fond to imagine
That, after this life, there is any pain?
No, these are trifles and mere old wives' tales.

MEPHIST. But I am an instance to prove the contrary,
For I tell thee I am damn'd and now in hell.

FAUSTUS. Nay, an this be hell, I'll willingly be damn'd:
What! sleeping, eating, walking, and disputing!
But, leaving this, let me have a wife,
The fairest maid in Germany;
For I am wanton and lascivious,

And cannot live without a wife.

MEPHIST. Well, Faustus, thou shalt have a wife.

[MEPHISTOPHILIS fetches in a WOMAN-DEVIL.]

FAUSTUS. What sight is this?

MEPHIST. Now, Faustus, wilt thou have a wife?

FAUSTUS. Here's a hot whore, indeed: no, I'll no wife.

MEPHIST. Marriage is but a ceremonial toy,
And, if thou lov'st me, think no more of it.
I'll cull thee out the fairest courtezans,
And bring them every morning to thy bed:
She whom thine eye shall like, thy heart shall have,
Were she as chaste as was Penelope,
As wise as Saba, or as beautiful
As was bright Lucifer before his fall.
Here, take this book, peruse it well:
The iterating of these lines brings gold;
The framing of this circle on the ground
Brings thunder, whirlwinds, storm, and lightning;
Pronounce this thrice devoutly to thyself,
And men in harness shall appear to thee,
Ready to execute what thou command'st.

FAUSTUS. Thanks, Mephistophilis, for this sweet book:
This will I keep as chary as my life.
    [Exeunt.]

Enter FAUSTUS, in his study, and MEPHISTOPHILIS.

FAUSTUS. When I behold the heavens, then I repent,
And curse thee, wicked Mephistophilis,
Because thou hast depriv'd me of those joys.

MEPHIST. 'Twas thine own seeking, Faustus; thank thyself.
But, think'st thou heaven is such a glorious thing?
I tell thee, Faustus, it is not half so fair
As thou, or any man that breathes on earth.

FAUSTUS. How prov'st thou that?

MEPHIST. 'Twas made for man; then he's more excellent.

FAUSTUS. If heaven was made for man, 'twas made for me:
I will renounce this magic and repent.

Enter GOOD ANGEL and EVIL ANGEL.

GOOD ANGEL. Faustus, repent; yet God will pity thee.

EVIL ANGEL. Thou art a spirit; God cannot pity thee.

FAUSTUS. Who buzzeth in mine ears I am a spirit?
Be I a devil, yet God may pity me;
Yea, God will pity me, if I repent.

EVIL ANGEL. Ay, but Faustus never shall repent.
    [Exeunt ANGELS.]

FAUSTUS. My heart is harden'd, I cannot repent;
Scarce can I name salvation, faith, or heaven:
Swords, poisons, halters, and envenom'd steel
Are laid before me to despatch myself;
And long ere this I should have done the deed,
Had not sweet pleasure conquer'd deep despair.
Have not I made blind Homer sing to me
Of Alexander's love and Oenon's death?
And hath not he, that built the walls of Thebes
With ravishing sound of his melodious harp,
Made music with my Mephistophilis?
Why should I die, then, or basely despair?
I am resolv'd; Faustus shall not repent.—
Come, Mephistophilis, let us dispute again,
And reason of divine astrology.
Speak, are there many spheres above the moon?
Are all celestial bodies but one globe,
As is the substance of this centric earth?

MEPHIST. As are the elements, such are the heavens,
Even from the moon unto th' empyreal orb,
Mutually folded in each other's spheres,
And jointly move upon one axletree,

Whose termine is term'd the world's wide pole;
Nor are the names of Saturn, Mars, or Jupiter
Feign'd, but are erring stars.

FAUSTUS. But have they all one motion, both situ et tempore?

MEPHIST. All move from east to west in four-and-twenty
hours upon the poles of the world; but differ in their motions
upon the poles of the zodiac.

FAUSTUS. These slender questions Wagner can decide:
Hath Mephistophilis no greater skill?
Who knows not the double motion of the planets?
That the first is finish'd in a natural day;
The second thus; Saturn in thirty years; Jupiter in twelve;
Mars in four; the Sun, Venus, and Mercury in a year; the Moon
in twenty-eight days. These are freshmen's questions. But
tell me, hath every sphere a dominion or intelligentia?

MEPHIST. Ay.

FAUSTUS. How many heavens or spheres are there?

MEPHIST. Nine; the seven planets, the firmament, and the empyreal
heaven.

FAUSTUS. But is there not coelum igneum et crystallinum?

MEPHIST. No, Faustus, they be but fables.

FAUSTUS. Resolve me, then, in this one question; why are not
conjunctions, oppositions, aspects, eclipses, all at one time,
but in some years we have more, in some less?

MEPHIST. Per inoequalem motum respectu totius.

FAUSTUS. Well, I am answered. Now tell me who made the world?

MEPHIST. I will not.

FAUSTUS. Sweet Mephistophilis, tell me.

MEPHIST. Move me not, Faustus.

FAUSTUS. Villain, have I not bound thee to tell me any thing?

MEPHIST. Ay, that is not against our kingdom; this is.
Thou art damned; think thou of hell.

FAUSTUS. Think, Faustus, upon God that made the world.

MEPHIST. Remember this.
  [Exit.]

FAUSTUS. Ay, go, accursed spirit, to ugly hell!
'Tis thou hast damn'd distressed Faustus' soul.
Is't not too late?

  Re-enter GOOD ANGEL and EVIL ANGEL.

EVIL ANGEL. Too late.

GOOD ANGEL. Never too late, if Faustus will repent.

EVIL ANGEL. If thou repent, devils will tear thee in pieces.

GOOD ANGEL. Repent, and they shall never raze thy skin.
  [Exeunt ANGELS.]

FAUSTUS. O Christ, my Saviour, my Saviour
Help to save distressed Faustus' soul!

  Enter LUCIFER, BELZEBUB, and MEPHISTOPHILIS.

LUCIFER. Christ cannot save thy soul, for he is just:
There's none but I have interest in the same.

FAUSTUS. O, what art thou that look'st so terribly?

LUCIFER. I am Lucifer,
And this is my companion-prince in hell.

FAUSTUS. O Faustus, they are come to fetch thy soul!

BELZEBUB. We are come to tell thee thou dost injure us.

LUCIFER. Thou call'st of Christ, contrary to thy promise.

BELZEBUB. Thou shouldst not think on God.

LUCIFER. Think of the devil.

BELZEBUB. And his dam too.

FAUSTUS. Nor will Faustus henceforth: pardon him for this,
And Faustus vows never to look to heaven.

LUCIFER. So shalt thou shew thyself an obedient servant,
And we will highly gratify thee for it.

BELZEBUB. Faustus, we are come from hell in person to shew thee
some pastime: sit down, and thou shalt behold the Seven Deadly
Sins appear to thee in their own proper shapes and likeness.

FAUSTUS. That sight will be as pleasant unto me,
As Paradise was to Adam the first day
Of his creation.

LUCIFER. Talk not of Paradise or creation; but mark the show.—
Go, Mephistophilis, and fetch them in.

MEPHISTOPHILIS brings in the SEVEN DEADLY SINS.

BELZEBUB. Now, Faustus, question them of their names and
dispositions.

FAUSTUS. That shall I soon.—What art thou, the first?

PRIDE. I am Pride. I disdain to have any parents. I am like to
Ovid's flea; I can creep into every corner of a wench; sometimes,
like a perriwig, I sit upon her brow; next, like a necklace, I hang
about her neck; then, like a fan of feathers, I kiss her lips;
and then, turning myself to a wrought smock, do what I list.
But, fie, what a smell is here! I'll not speak a word more for
a king's ransom, unless the ground be perfumed, and covered with
cloth of arras.

FAUSTUS. Thou art a proud knave, indeed.—What art thou, the second?

COVETOUSNESS. I am Covetousness, begotten of an old churl, in a leather bag: and, might I now obtain my wish, this house, you, and all, should turn to gold, that I might lock you safe into my chest: O my sweet gold!

FAUSTUS. And what art thou, the third?

ENVY. I am Envy, begotten of a chimney-sweeper and an oyster-wife. I cannot read, and therefore wish all books burned. I am lean with seeing others eat. O, that there would come a famine over all the world, that all might die, and I live alone! then thou shouldst see how fat I'd be. But must thou sit, and I stand? come down, with a vengeance!

FAUSTUS. Out, envious wretch!—But what art thou, the fourth?

WRATH. I am Wrath. I had neither father nor mother: I leapt out of a lion's mouth when I was scarce an hour old; and ever since have run up and down the world with this case of rapiers, wounding myself when I could get none to fight withal. I was born in hell; and look to it, for some of you shall be my father.

FAUSTUS. And what art thou, the fifth?

GLUTTONY. I am Gluttony. My parents are all dead, and the devil a penny they have left me, but a small pension, and that buys me thirty meals a-day and ten bevers,—a small trifle to suffice nature. I come of a royal pedigree: my father was a Gammonof Bacon, my mother was a Hogshead of Claret-wine; my godfathers were these, Peter Pickled-herring and Martin Martlemas-beef; but my godmother, O, she was an ancient gentlewoman; her name was Margery March-beer. Now, Faustus, thou hast heard all my progeny; wilt thou bid me to supper?

FAUSTUS. Not I.

GLUTTONY. Then the devil choke thee!

FAUSTUS. Choke thyself, glutton!—What art thou, the sixth?

SLOTH. Heigho! I am Sloth. I was begotten on a sunny bank. Heigho! I'll not speak a word more for a king's ransom.

FAUSTUS. And what are you, Mistress Minx, the seventh and last?

LECHERY. Who, I, sir? I am one that loves an inch of raw mutton better than an ell of fried stock-fish; and the first letter of my name begins with L.

LUCIFER. Away to hell, away! On, piper!
    [Exeunt the SINS.]

FAUSTUS. O, how this sight doth delight my soul!

LUCIFER. Tut, Faustus, in hell is all manner of delight.

FAUSTUS. O, might I see hell, and return again safe,
How happy were I then!

LUCIFER. Faustus, thou shalt; at midnight I will send for thee.
Meanwhile peruse this book and view it throughly,
And thou shalt turn thyself into what shape thou wilt.

FAUSTUS. Thanks, mighty Lucifer!
This will I keep as chary as my life.

LUCIFER. Now, Faustus, farewell.

FAUSTUS. Farewell, great Lucifer.
    [Exeunt LUCIFER and BELZEBUB.]

Come, Mephistophilis.
    [Exeunt.]

    Enter ROBIN, with a book.

ROBIN. What, Dick! look to the horses there, till I come again.
I have gotten one of Doctor Faustus' conjuring-books; and now
we'll have such knavery as't passes.

    Enter DICK.

DICK. What, Robin! you must come away and walk the horses.

ROBIN. I walk the horses! I scorn't, faith I have other
matters in hand: let the horses walk themselves, an they will.—

[Reads.]
A per se, a; t, h, e, the; o per se, o; Demy orgon gorgon.—
Keep further from me, O thou illiterate and unlearned hostler!

DICK. 'Snails, what hast thou got there? a book! why, thou canst
not tell ne'er a word on't.

ROBIN. That thou shalt see presently: keep out of the circle,
I say, lest I send you into the ostry with a vengeance.

DICK. That's like, faith! you had best leave your foolery; for,
an my master come, he'll conjure you, faith.

ROBIN. My master conjure me! I'll tell thee what; an my master
come here, I'll clap as fair a pair of horns on's head as
e'er thou sawest in thy life.

DICK. Thou need'st not do that, for my mistress hath done it.

ROBIN. Ay, there be of us here that have waded as deep into
matters as other men, if they were disposed to talk.

DICK. A plague take you! I thought you did not sneak up and down after
her for nothing. But, I prithee, tell me in good sadness,
Robin, is that a conjuring-book?

ROBIN. Do but speak what thou'lt have me to do, and I'll do't:
if thou'lt dance naked, put off thy clothes, and I'll conjure
thee about presently; or, if thou'lt go but to the tavern with
me, I'll give thee white wine, red wine, claret-wine, sack,
muscadine, malmsey, and whippincrust, hold, belly, hold; and
we'll not pay one penny for it.

DICK. O, brave! Prithee, let's to it presently, for I am as
dry as a dog.

ROBIN. Come, then, let's away.
    [Exeunt.]

    Enter CHORUS.

CHORUS. Learned Faustus,
To find the secrets of astronomy

Graven in the book of Jove's high firmament,
Did mount him up to scale Olympus' top;
Where, sitting in a chariot burning bright,
Drawn by the strength of yoked dragons' necks,
He views the clouds, the planets, and the stars,
The tropic zones, and quarters of the sky,
From the bright circle of the horned moon
Even to the height of Primum Mobile;
And, whirling round with this circumference,
Within the concave compass of the pole,
From east to west his dragons swiftly glide,
And in eight days did bring him home again.
Not long he stay'd within his quiet house,
To rest his bones after his weary toil;
But new exploits do hale him out again:
And, mounted then upon a dragon's back,
That with his wings did part the subtle air,
He now is gone to prove cosmography,
That measures coasts and kingdoms of the earth;
And, as I guess, will first arrive at Rome,
To see the Pope and manner of his court,
And take some part of holy Peter's feast,
The which this day is highly solemniz'd.
        [Exit.]

        Enter FAUSTUS and MEPHISTOPHILIS.

FAUSTUS. Having now, my good Mephistophilis,
Pass'd with delight the stately town of Trier,
Environ'd round with airy mountain-tops,
With walls of flint, and deep-entrenched lakes,
Not to be won by any conquering prince;
From Paris next, coasting the realm of France,
We saw the river Maine fall into Rhine,
Whose banks are set with groves of fruitful vines;
Then up to Naples, rich Campania,
Whose buildings fair and gorgeous to the eye,
The streets straight forth, and pav'd with finest brick,
Quarter the town in four equivalents:
There saw we learned Maro's golden tomb;
The way he cut, an English mile in length,
Thorough a rock of stone, in one night's space;
From thence to Venice, Padua, and the rest,

In one of which a sumptuous temple stands,
That threats the stars with her aspiring top,
Whose frame is pav'd with sundry-colour'd stones,
And roof'd aloft with curious work in gold.
Thus hitherto hath Faustus spent his time:
But tell me now, what resting-place is this?
Hast thou, as erst I did command,
Conducted me within the walls of Rome?

MEPHIST. I have, my Faustus; and, for proof thereof,
This is the goodly palace of the Pope;
And, 'cause we are no common guests,
I choose his privy-chamber for our use.

FAUSTUS. I hope his Holiness will bid us welcome.

MEPHIST. All's one, for we'll be bold with his venison.
But now, my Faustus, that thou mayst perceive
What Rome contains for to delight thine eyes,
Know that this city stands upon seven hills
That underprop the groundwork of the same:
Just through the midst runs flowing Tiber's stream,
With winding banks that cut it in two parts;
Over the which two stately bridges lean,
That make safe passage to each part of Rome:
Upon the bridge call'd Ponte Angelo
Erected is a castle passing strong,
Where thou shalt see such store of ordnance,
As that the double cannons, forg'd of brass,
Do match the number of the days contain'd
Within the compass of one complete year;
Beside the gates, and high pyramides,
That Julius Caesar brought from Africa.

FAUSTUS. Now, by the kingdoms of infernal rule,
Of Styx, of Acheron, and the fiery lake
Of ever-burning Phlegethon, I swear
That I do long to see the monuments
And situation of bright-splendent Rome:
Come, therefore, let's away.

MEPHIST. Nay, stay, my Faustus: I know you'd see the Pope,
And take some part of holy Peter's feast,

The which, in state and high solemnity,
This day, is held through Rome and Italy,
In honour of the Pope's triumphant victory.

FAUSTUS. Sweet Mephistophilis, thou pleasest me.
Whilst I am here on earth, let me be cloy'd
With all things that delight the heart of man:
My four-and-twenty years of liberty
I'll spend in pleasure and in dalliance,
That Faustus' name, whilst this bright frame doth stand,
May be admir'd thorough the furthest land.

MEPHIST. 'Tis well said, Faustus. Come, then, stand by me,
And thou shalt see them come immediately.

FAUSTUS. Nay, stay, my gentle Mephistophilis,
And grant me my request, and then I go.
Thou know'st, within the compass of eight days
We view'd the face of heaven, of earth, and hell;
So high our dragons soar'd into the air,
That, looking down, the earth appear'd to me
No bigger than my hand in quantity;
There did we view the kingdoms of the world,
And what might please mine eye I there beheld.
Then in this show let me an actor be,
That this proud Pope may Faustus' cunning see.

MEPHIST. Let it be so, my Faustus. But, first, stay,
And view their triumphs as they pass this way;
And then devise what best contents thy mind,
By cunning in thine art to cross the Pope,
Or dash the pride of this solemnity;
To make his monks and abbots stand like apes,
And point like antics at his triple crown;
To beat the beads about the friars' pates,
Or clap huge horns upon the Cardinals' heads;
Or any villany thou canst devise;
And I'll perform it, Faustus. Hark! they come:
This day shall make thee be admir'd in Rome.

  Enter the CARDINALS and BISHOPS, some bearing crosiers, some
the pillars; MONKS and FRIARS, singing their procession;

then the POPE, RAYMOND king of Hungary, the ARCHBISHOP
OF RHEIMS, BRUNO led in chains, and ATTENDANTS.

POPE. Cast down our footstool.

RAYMOND. Saxon Bruno, stoop,
Whilst on thy back his Holiness ascends
Saint Peter's chair and state pontifical.

BRUNO. Proud Lucifer, that state belongs to me;
But thus I fall to Peter, not to thee.

POPE. To me and Peter shalt thou grovelling lie,
And crouch before the Papal dignity.—
Sound trumpets, then; for thus Saint Peter's heir,
From Bruno's back, ascends Saint Peter's chair.
    [A flourish while he ascends.]
Thus, as the gods creep on with feet of wool,
Long ere with iron hands they punish men,
So shall our sleeping vengeance now arise,
And smite with death thy hated enterprise.
Lord Cardinals of France and Padua,
Go forthwith to our holy consistory,
And read, amongst the statutes decretal,
What, by the holy council held at Trent,
The sacred synod hath decreed for him
That doth assume the Papal government
Without election and a true consent:
Away, and bring us word with speed.

CARDINAL OF FRANCE. We go, my lord.
    [Exeunt CARDINALS of France and Padua.]

POPE. Lord Raymond.
    [They converse in dumb show.]

FAUSTUS. Go, haste thee, gentle Mephistophilis,
Follow the cardinals to the consistory;
And, as they turn their superstitious books,
Strike them with sloth and drowsy idleness,
And make them sleep so sound, that in their shapes
Thyself and I may parley with this Pope,
This proud confronter of the Emperor;

And, in despite of all his holiness,
Restore this Bruno to his liberty,
And bear him to the states of Germany.

MEPHIST. Faustus, I go.

FAUSTUS. Despatch it soon:
The Pope shall curse, that Faustus came to Rome.
    [Exeunt FAUSTUS and MEPHISTOPHILIS.]

BRUNO. Pope Adrian, let me have right of law:
I was elected by the Emperor.

POPE. We will depose the Emperor for that deed,
And curse the people that submit to him:
Both he and thou shall stand excommunicate,
And interdict from church's privilege
And all society of holy men.
He grows too proud in his authority,
Lifting his lofty head above the clouds,
And, like a steeple, overpeers the church:
But we'll pull down his haughty insolence;
And, as Pope Alexander, our progenitor,
Trod on the neck of German Frederick,
Adding this golden sentence to our praise,
"That Peter's heirs should tread on Emperors,
And walk upon the dreadful adder's back,
Treading the lion and the dragon down,
And fearless spurn the killing basilisk,"
So will we quell that haughty schismatic,
And, by authority apostolical,
Depose him from his regal government.

BRUNO. Pope Julius swore to princely Sigismond,
For him and the succeeding Popes of Rome,
To hold the Emperors their lawful lords.

POPE. Pope Julius did abuse the church's rights,
And therefore none of his decrees can stand.
Is not all power on earth bestow'd on us?
And therefore, though we would, we cannot err.
Behold this silver belt, whereto is fix'd
Seven golden seals, fast sealed with seven seals,

In token of our seven-fold power from heaven,
To bind or loose, lock fast, condemn or judge,
Resign or seal, or what so pleaseth us:
Then he and thou, and all the world, shall stoop,
Or be assured of our dreadful curse,
To light as heavy as the pains of hell.

Re-enter FAUSTUS and MEPHISTOPHILIS, in the shapes of the CARDINALS of France and Padua.

MEPHIST. Now tell me, Faustus, are we not fitted well?

FAUSTUS. Yes, Mephistophilis; and two such cardinals
Ne'er serv'd a holy Pope as we shall do.
But, whilst they sleep within the consistory,
Let us salute his reverend fatherhood.

RAYMOND. Behold, my lord, the Cardinals are return'd.

POPE. Welcome, grave fathers: answer presently
What hath our holy council there decreed
Concerning Bruno and the Emperor,
In quittance of their late conspiracy
Against our state and papal dignity?

FAUSTUS. Most sacred patron of the church of Rome,
By full consent of all the synod
Of priests and prelates, it is thus decreed,—
That Bruno and the German Emperor
Be held as Lollards and bold schismatics,
And proud disturbers of the church's peace;
And if that Bruno, by his own assent,
Without enforcement of the German peers,
Did seek to wear the triple diadem,
And by your death to climb Saint Peter's chair,
The statutes decretal have thus decreed,—
He shall be straight condemn'd of heresy,
And on a pile of faggots burnt to death.

POPE. It is enough. Here, take him to your charge,
And bear him straight to Ponte Angelo,
And in the strongest tower enclose him fast.
To-morrow, sitting in our consistory,

With all our college of grave cardinals,
We will determine of his life or death.
Here, take his triple crown along with you,
And leave it in the church's treasury.
Make haste again, my good Lord Cardinals,
And take our blessing apostolical.

MEPHIST. So, so; was never devil thus bless'd before.

FAUSTUS. Away, sweet Mephistophilis, be gone;
The Cardinals will be plagu'd for this anon.
    [Exeunt FAUSTUS and MEPHISTOPHILIS with BRUNO.]

POPE. Go presently and bring a banquet forth,
That we may solemnize Saint Peter's feast,
And with Lord Raymond, King of Hungary,
Drink to our late and happy victory.

    A Sennet while the banquet is brought in; and then enter
    FAUSTUS and MEPHISTOPHILIS in their own shapes.

MEPHIST. Now, Faustus, come, prepare thyself for mirth:
The sleepy Cardinals are hard at hand,
To censure Bruno, that is posted hence,
And on a proud-pac'd steed, as swift as thought,
Flies o'er the Alps to fruitful Germany,
There to salute the woful Emperor.

FAUSTUS. The Pope will curse them for their sloth to-day,
That slept both Bruno and his crown away.
But now, that Faustus may delight his mind,
And by their folly make some merriment,
Sweet Mephistophilis, so charm me here,
That I may walk invisible to all,
And do whate'er I please, unseen of any.

MEPHIST. Faustus, thou shalt: then kneel down presently,
Whilst on thy head I lay my hand,
And charm thee with this magic wand.
First, wear this girdle; then appear
Invisible to all are here:
The planets seven, the gloomy air,
Hell, and the Furies' forked hair,

Pluto's blue fire, and Hecat's tree,
With magic spells so compass thee,
That no eye may thy body see!
So, Faustus, now, for all their holiness,
Do what thou wilt, thou shalt not be discern'd.

FAUSTUS. Thanks, Mephistophilis.—Now, friars, take heed,
Lest Faustus make your shaven crowns to bleed.

MEPHIST. Faustus, no more: see, where the Cardinals come!

Re-enter the CARDINALS of France and Padua with a book.

POPE. Welcome, Lord Cardinals; come, sit down.—
Lord Raymond, take your seat.—Friars, attend,
And see that all things be in readiness,
As best beseems this solemn festival.

CARDINAL OF FRANCE. First, may it please your sacred Holiness
To view the sentence of the reverend synod
Concerning Bruno and the Emperor?

POPE. What needs this question? did I not tell you,
To-morrow we would sit i' the consistory,
And there determine of his punishment?
You brought us word even now, it was decreed
That Bruno and the cursed Emperor
Were by the holy council both condemn'd
For loathed Lollards and base schismatics:
Then wherefore would you have me view that book?

CARDINAL OF FRANCE. Your grace mistakes; you gave us no such
charge.

RAYMOND. Deny it not; we all are witnesses
That Bruno here was late deliver'd you,
With his rich triple crown to be reserv'd
And put into the church's treasury.

BOTH CARDINALS. By holy Paul, we saw them not!

POPE. By Peter, you shall die,
Unless you bring them forth immediately!—

Hale them to prison, lade their limbs with gyves.—
False prelates, for this hateful treachery
Curs'd be your souls to hellish misery!
    [Exeunt ATTENDANTS with the two CARDINALS.]

FAUSTUS. So, they are safe. Now, Faustus, to the feast:
The Pope had never such a frolic guest.

POPE. Lord Archbishop of Rheims, sit down with us.

ARCHBISHOP. I thank your Holiness.

FAUSTUS. Fall to; the devil choke you, an you spare!

POPE. Who is that spoke?—Friars, look about.—
Lord Raymond, pray, fall to. I am beholding
To the Bishop of Milan for this so rare a present.

FAUSTUS. I thank you, sir.
    [Snatches the dish.]

POPE. How now! who snatch'd the meat from me?
Villains, why speak you not?—
My good Lord Archbishop, here's a most dainty dish
Was sent me from a cardinal in France.

FAUSTUS. I'll have that too.
    [Snatches the dish.]

POPE. What Lollards do attend our holiness,
That we receive such great indignity?
Fetch me some wine.

FAUSTUS. Ay, pray, do, for Faustus is a-dry.

POPE. Lord Raymond,
I drink unto your grace.

FAUSTUS. I pledge your grace.
    [Snatches the cup.]

POPE. My wine gone too!—Ye lubbers, look about,
And find the man that doth this villany,

37

Or, by our sanctitude, you all shall die!—
I pray, my lords, have patience at this
Troublesome banquet.

ARCHBISHOP. Please it your Holiness, I think it be some ghost crept out of Purgatory, and now is come unto your Holiness for his pardon.

POPE. It may be so.—
Go, then, command our priests to sing a dirge,
To lay the fury of this same troublesome ghost.
    [Exit an ATTENDANT.—The POPE crosses himself.]

FAUSTUS. How now! must every bit be spic'd with a cross?—
Nay, then, take that.
    [Strikes the POPE.]

POPE. O, I am slain!—Help me, my lords!
O, come and help to bear my body hence!—
Damn'd be his soul for ever for this deed!
    [Exeunt all except FAUSTUS and MEPHISTOPHILIS.]

MEPHIST. Now, Faustus, what will you do now? for I can tell you you'll be cursed with bell, book, and candle.

FAUSTUS. Bell, book, and candle,—candle, book, and bell,—
Forward and backward, to curse Faustus to hell!

    Re-enter the FRIARS, with bell, book, and candle, for the
    Dirge.

FIRST FRIAR. Come, brethren, lets about our business with good devotion.
    [They sing.]

CURSED BE HE THAT STOLE HIS HOLINESS' MEAT FROM THE TABLE! maledicat Dominus! CURSED BE HE THAT STRUCK HIS HOLINESS A BLOW ON THE FACE! maledicat Dominus! CURSED BE HE THAT STRUCK FRIAR SANDELO A BLOW ON THE PATE! maledicat Dominus! CURSED BE HE THAT DISTURBETH OUR HOLY DIRGE! Maledicat Dominus!
CURSED BE HE THAT TOOK AWAY HIS HOLINESS' WINE! Maledicat Dominus!

[MEPHISTOPHILIS and FAUSTUS beat the FRIARS, and fling fire-works among them, and exeunt.]

Enter ROBIN and DICK with a cup.

DICK. Sirrah Robin, we were best look that your devil can answer the stealing of this same cup, for the Vintner's boy follows us at the hard heels.

ROBIN. 'Tis no matter; let him come: an he follow us, I'll so conjure him as he was never conjured in his life, I warrant him. Let me see the cup.

DICK. Here 'tis.
    [Gives the cup to ROBIN.]
Yonder he comes: now, Robin, now or never shew thy cunning.

    Enter VINTNER.

VINTNER. O, are you here? I am glad I have found you. You are a couple of fine companions: pray, where's the cup you stole from the tavern?

ROBIN. How, how! we steal a cup! take heed what you say: we look not like cup-stealers, I can tell you.

VINTNER. Never deny't, for I know you have it; and I'll search you.

ROBIN. Search me! ay, and spare not.
—Hold the cup, Dick [Aside to DICK, giving him the cup].—
Come, come, search me, search me.

    [VINTNER searches him.]

VINTNER. Come on, sirrah, let me search you now.

DICK. Ay, ay, do, do.
—Hold the cup, Robin [Aside to ROBIN, giving him the cup].—
I fear not your searching: we scorn to steal your cups,
I can tell you.

    [VINTNER searches him.]

VINTNER. Never out-face me for the matter; for, sure, the cup is between you two.

ROBIN. Nay, there you lie; 'tis beyond us both.

VINTNER. A plague take you! I thought 'twas your knavery to take it away: come, give it me again.

ROBIN. Ay, much! when, can you tell?—Dick, make me a circle, and stand close at my back, and stir not for thy life.—Vintner, you shall have your cup anon.—Say nothing, Dick.—[Reads from a book] O per se, O; Demogorgon; Belcher, and Mephistophilis!

    Enter MEPHISTOPHILIS.

MEPHIST. You princely legions of infernal rule,
How am I vexed by these villains' charms!
From Constantinople have they brought me now,
Only for pleasure of these damned slaves.
   [Exit VINTNER.]

ROBIN. By lady, sir, you have had a shrewd journey of it! will it please you to take a shoulder of mutton to supper, and a tester in your purse, and go back again?

DICK. Ay, I pray you heartily, sir; for we called you but in jest, I promise you.

MEPHIST. To purge the rashness of this cursed deed,
First, be thou turned to this ugly shape,
For apish deeds transformed to an ape.

ROBIN. O, brave! an ape! I pray, sir, let me have the carrying of him about, to shew some tricks.

MEPHIST. And so thou shalt: be thou transformed to a dog, and carry him upon thy back. Away! be gone!

ROBIN. A dog! that's excellent: let the maids look well to their porridge-pots, for I'll into the kitchen presently.—Come, Dick, come.
   [Exeunt ROBIN and DICK.]

MEPHIST. Now with the flames of ever-burning fire
I'll wing myself, and forthwith fly amain
Unto my Faustus, to the Great Turk's court.
    [Exit.]

Enter MARTINO and FREDERICK at several doors.

MARTINO. What, ho, officers, gentlemen!
Hie to the presence to attend the Emperor.—
Good Frederick, see the rooms be voided straight:
His majesty is coming to the hall;
Go back, and see the state in readiness.

FREDERICK. But where is Bruno, our elected Pope,
That on a Fury's back came post from Rome?
Will not his grace consort the Emperor?

MARTINO. O, yes; and with him comes the German conjurer,
The learned Faustus, fame of Wittenberg,
The wonder of the world for magic art;
And he intends to shew great Carolus
The race of all his stout progenitors,
And bring in presence of his majesty
The royal shapes and perfect semblances
Of Alexander and his beauteous paramour.

FREDERICK. Where is Benvolio?

MARTINO. Fast asleep, I warrant you;
He took his rouse with stoops of Rhenish wine
So kindly yesternight to Bruno's health,
That all this day the sluggard keeps his bed.

FREDERICK. See, see, his window's ope! we'll call to him.

MARTINO. What, ho! Benvolio!

Enter BENVOLIO above, at a window, in his nightcap, buttoning.

BENVOLIO. What a devil ail you two?

MARTINO. Speak softly, sir, lest the devil hear you;
For Faustus at the court is late arriv'd,

And at his heels a thousand Furies wait,
To accomplish whatsoe'er the doctor please.

BENVOLIO. What of this?

MARTINO. Come, leave thy chamber first, and thou shalt see
This conjurer perform such rare exploits,
Before the Pope and royal Emperor,
As never yet was seen in Germany.

BENVOLIO. Has not the Pope enough of conjuring yet?
He was upon the devil's back late enough:
An if he be so far in love with him,
I would he would post with him to Rome again!

FREDERICK. Speak, wilt thou come and see this sport?

BENVOLIO. Not I.

MARTINO. Wilt thou stand in thy window, and see it, then?

BENVOLIO. Ay, an I fall not asleep i' the mean time.

MARTINO. The Emperor is at hand, who comes to see
What wonders by black spells may compass'd be.

BENVOLIO. Well, go you attend the Emperor. I am content, for
this once, to thrust my head out at a window; for they
say, if a man be drunk over night, the devil cannot hurt him
in the morning: if that be true, I have a charm in my head,
shall control him as well as the conjurer, I warrant you.
      [Exeunt FREDERICK and MARTINO.]

      A Sennet. Enter CHARLES the German Emperor, BRUNO,
      DUKE OF SAXONY, FAUSTUS, MEPHISTOPHILIS,
FREDERICK, MARTINO, and Attendants.

EMPEROR. Wonder of men, renowm'd magician,
Thrice-learned Faustus, welcome to our court.
This deed of thine, in setting Bruno free
From his and our professed enemy,
Shall add more excellence unto thine art
Than if by powerful necromantic spells

Thou couldst command the world's obedience:
For ever be belov'd of Carolus!
And if this Bruno, thou hast late redeem'd,
In peace possess the triple diadem,
And sit in Peter's chair, despite of chance,
Thou shalt be famous through all Italy,
And honour'd of the German Emperor.

FAUSTUS. These gracious words, most royal Carolus,
Shall make poor Faustus, to his utmost power,
Both love and serve the German Emperor,
And lay his life at holy Bruno's feet:
For proof whereof, if so your grace be pleas'd,
The doctor stands prepar'd by power of art
To cast his magic charms, that shall pierce through
The ebon gates of ever-burning hell,
And hale the stubborn Furies from their caves,
To compass whatsoe'er your grace commands.

BENVOLIO. Blood, he speaks terribly! but, for all that, I do not
greatly believe him: he looks as like a conjurer as the Pope
to a costermonger. [Aside.]

EMPEROR. Then, Faustus, as thou late didst promise us,
We would behold that famous conqueror,
Great Alexander, and his paramour,
In their true shapes and state majestical,
That we may wonder at their excellence.

FAUSTUS. Your majesty shall see them presently.—
Mephistophilis, away,
And, with a solemn noise of trumpets' sound,
Present before this royal Emperor
Great Alexander and his beauteous paramour.

MEPHIST. Faustus, I will.
    [Exit.]

BENVOLIO. Well, Master Doctor, an your devils come not away
quickly, you shall have me asleep presently: zounds, I could
eat myself for anger, to think I have been such an ass all this
while, to stand gaping after the devil's governor, and can see
nothing!

FAUSTUS.
I'll make you feel something anon, if my art fail me not.—
My lord, I must forewarn your majesty,
That, when my spirits present the royal shapes
Of Alexander and his paramour,
Your grace demand no questions of the king,
But in dumb silence let them come and go.

EMPEROR. Be it as Faustus please; we are content.

BENVOLIO. Ay, ay, and I am content too: an thou bring Alexander
and his paramour before the Emperor, I'll be Actaeon, and turn
myself to a stag.

FAUSTUS. And I'll play Diana, and send you the horns presently.

> Sennet. Enter, at one door, the EMPEROR ALEXANDER, at the
> other, DARIUS. They meet. DARIUS is thrown down;
> ALEXANDER kills him, takes off his crown, and, offering to go out,
> his PARAMOUR meets him. He embraceth her, and sets DARIUS'
> crown upon her head; and, coming back, both salute the EMPEROR,
> who, leaving his state, offers to embrace them; which FAUSTUS
> seeing, suddenly stays him. Then trumpets cease, and music sounds.

My gracious lord, you do forget yourself;
These are but shadows, not substantial.

EMPEROR. O, pardon me! my thoughts are so ravish'd
With sight of this renowmed emperor,
That in mine arms I would have compass'd him.
But, Faustus, since I may not speak to them,
To satisfy my longing thoughts at full,
Let me this tell thee: I have heard it said
That this fair lady, whilst she liv'd on earth,
Had on her neck a little wart or mole;
How may I prove that saying to be true?

FAUSTUS. Your majesty may boldly go and see.

EMPEROR. Faustus, I see it plain;
And in this sight thou better pleasest me
Than if I gain'd another monarchy.

FAUSTUS. Away! be gone! [Exit show.]—See, see, my gracious
lord! what strange beast is yon, that thrusts his head out at
window?

EMPEROR. O, wondrous sight!—See, Duke of Saxony,
Two spreading horns most strangely fastened
Upon the head of young Benvolio!

SAXONY. What, is he asleep or dead?

FAUSTUS. He sleeps, my lord; but dreams not of his horns.

EMPEROR. This sport is excellent: we'll call and wake him.—
What, ho, Benvolio!

BENVOLIO. A plague upon you! let me sleep a while.

EMPEROR. I blame thee not to sleep much, having such a head of
thine own.

SAXONY. Look up, Benvolio; 'tis the Emperor calls.

BENVOLIO. The Emperor! where?—O, zounds, my head!

EMPEROR. Nay, an thy horns hold, 'tis no matter for thy head,
for that's armed sufficiently.

FAUSTUS. Why, how now, Sir Knight! what, hanged by the horns!
this is most horrible: fie, fie, pull in your head, for
shame! let not all the world wonder at you.

BENVOLIO. Zounds, doctor, this is your villany!

FAUSTUS. O, say not so, sir! the doctor has no skill,
No art, no cunning, to present these lords,
Or bring before this royal Emperor
The mighty monarch, warlike Alexander.
If Faustus do it, you are straight resolv'd,
In bold Actaeon's shape, to turn a stag:—
And therefore, my lord, so please your majesty,
I'll raise a kennel of hounds shall hunt him so
As all his footmanship shall scarce prevail

To keep his carcass from their bloody fangs.—
Ho, Belimoth, Argiron, Asteroth!

BENVOLIO. Hold, hold!—Zounds, he'll raise up a kennel of devils, I
think, anon.—Good my lord, entreat for me.—'Sblood, I am never able to
endure these torments.

EMPEROR. Then, good Master Doctor,
Let me entreat you to remove his horns;
He has done penance now sufficiently.

FAUSTUS. My gracious lord, not so much for injury done to me,
as to delight your majesty with some mirth, hath Faustus justly
requited this injurious knight; which being all I desire, I am
content to remove his horns.—Mephistophilis, transform him
[MEPHISTOPHILIS removes the horns]:—and hereafter, sir,
look you speak well of scholars.

BENVOLIO. Speak well of ye! 'sblood, an scholars be such
cuckold-makers, to clap horns of honest men's heads o' this
order, I'll ne'er trust smooth faces and small ruffs more.—But,
an I be not revenged for this, would I might be turned to a
gaping oyster, and drink nothing but salt water!
    [Aside, and then exit above.]

EMPEROR. Come, Faustus: while the Emperor lives,
In recompense of this thy high desert,
Thou shalt command the state of Germany,
And live belov'd of mighty Carolus.
    [Exeunt.]

Enter BENVOLIO, MARTINO, FREDERICK, and SOLDIERS.

MARTINO. Nay, sweet Benvolio, let us sway thy thoughts
From this attempt against the conjurer.

BENVOLIO. Away! you love me not, to urge me thus:
Shall I let slip so great an injury,
When every servile groom jests at my wrongs,
And in their rustic gambols proudly say,
"Benvolio's head was grac'd with horns today?"
O, may these eyelids never close again,
Till with my sword I have that conjurer slain!

If you will aid me in this enterprise,
Then draw your weapons and be resolute;
If not, depart: here will Benvolio die,
But Faustus' death shall quit my infamy.

FREDERICK. Nay, we will stay with thee, betide what may,
And kill that doctor, if he come this way.

BENVOLIO. Then, gentle Frederick, hie thee to the grove,
And place our servants and our followers
Close in an ambush there behind the trees.
By this, I know the conjurer is near:
I saw him kneel, and kiss the Emperor's hand,
And take his leave, laden with rich rewards.
Then, soldiers, boldly fight: if Faustus die,
Take you the wealth, leave us the victory.

FREDERICK. Come, soldiers, follow me unto the grove:
Who kills him shall have gold and endless love.
    [Exit FREDERICK with SOLDIERS.]

BENVOLIO. My head is lighter, than it was, by the horns;
But yet my heart's more ponderous than my head,
And pants until I see that conjurer dead.

MARTINO. Where shall we place ourselves, Benvolio?

BENVOLIO. Here will we stay to bide the first assault:
O, were that damned hell-hound but in place,
Thou soon shouldst see me quit my foul disgrace!

    Re-enter FREDERICK.

FREDERICK. Close, close! the conjurer is at hand,
And all alone comes walking in his gown;
Be ready, then, and strike the peasant down.

BENVOLIO. Mine be that honour, then. Now, sword, strike home!
For horns he gave I'll have his head anon.

MARTINO. See, see, he comes!

    Enter FAUSTUS with a false head.

BENVOLIO. No words. This blow ends all:
Hell take his soul! his body thus must fall.
 [Stabs FAUSTUS.]

FAUSTUS. [falling.] O!

FREDERICK. Groan you, Master Doctor?

BENVOLIO. Break may his heart with groans!—Dear Frederick, see,
Thus will I end his griefs immediately.

MARTINO. Strike with a willing hand.
 [BENVOLIO strikes off FAUSTUS' head.]
    His head is off.

BENVOLIO. The devil's dead; the Furies now may laugh.

FREDERICK. Was this that stern aspect, that awful frown,
Made the grim monarch of infernal spirits
Tremble and quake at his commanding charms?

MARTINO. Was this that damned head, whose art conspir'd
Benvolio's shame before the Emperor?

BENVOLIO. Ay, that's the head, and there the body lies,
Justly rewarded for his villanies.

FREDERICK. Come, let's devise how we may add more shame
To the black scandal of his hated name.

BENVOLIO. First, on his head, in quittance of my wrongs,
I'll nail huge forked horns, and let them hang
Within the window where he yok'd me first,
That all the world may see my just revenge.

MARTINO. What use shall we put his beard to?

BENVOLIO. We'll sell it to a chimney-sweeper: it will wear out
ten birchen brooms, I warrant you.

FREDERICK. What shall his eyes do?

BENVOLIO. We'll pull out his eyes; and they shall serve for
buttons to his lips, to keep his tongue from catching cold.

MARTINO. An excellent policy! and now, sirs, having divided him,
what shall the body do?
     [FAUSTUS rises.]

BENVOLIO. Zounds, the devil's alive again!

FREDERICK. Give him his head, for God's sake.

FAUSTUS. Nay, keep it: Faustus will have heads and hands,
Ay, all your hearts to recompense this deed.
Knew you not, traitors, I was limited
For four-and-twenty years to breathe on earth?
And, had you cut my body with your swords,
Or hew'd this flesh and bones as small as sand,
Yet in a minute had my spirit return'd,
And I had breath'd a man, made free from harm.
But wherefore do I dally my revenge?—
Asteroth, Belimoth, Mephistophilis?

     Enter MEPHISTOPHILIS, and other Devils.

Go, horse these traitors on your fiery backs,
And mount aloft with them as high as heaven:
Thence pitch them headlong to the lowest hell.
Yet, stay: the world shall see their misery,
And hell shall after plague their treachery.
Go, Belimoth, and take this caitiff hence,
And hurl him in some lake of mud and dirt.
Take thou this other, drag him through the woods
Amongst the pricking thorns and sharpest briers;
Whilst, with my gentle Mephistophilis,
This traitor flies unto some steepy rock,
That, rolling down, may break the villain's bones,
As he intended to dismember me.
Fly hence; despatch my charge immediately.

FREDERICK. Pity us, gentle Faustus! save our lives!

FAUSTUS. Away!

FREDERICK. He must needs go that the devil drives.
[Exeunt MEPHISTOPHILIS and DEVILS with BENVOLIO,
MARTINO, and FREDERICK.]

Enter the ambushed SOLDIERS.

FIRST SOLDIER. Come, sirs, prepare yourselves in readiness;
Make haste to help these noble gentlemen:
I heard them parley with the conjurer.

SECOND SOLDIER. See, where he comes! despatch and kill the slave.

FAUSTUS. What's here? an ambush to betray my life!
Then, Faustus, try thy skill.—Base peasants, stand!
For, lo, these trees remove at my command,
And stand as bulwarks 'twixt yourselves and me,
To shield me from your hated treachery!
Yet, to encounter this your weak attempt,
Behold, an army comes incontinent!

FAUSTUS strikes the door, and enter a DEVIL playing
on a drum; after him another, bearing an ensign; and divers
with weapons; MEPHISTOPHILIS with fire-works. They set   upon
the SOLDIERS, drive them out, and exeunt.

Enter, at several doors, BENVOLIO, FREDERICK, and MARTINO,
their heads and faces bloody, and besmeared with mud and dirt; all having
horns on their heads.

MARTINO. What, ho, Benvolio!

BENVOLIO. Here.—What, Frederick, ho!

FREDERICK. O, help me, gentle friend!—Where is Martino?

MARTINO. Dear Frederick, here,
Half smother'd in a lake of mud and dirt,
Through which the Furies dragg'd me by the heels.

FREDERICK. Martino, see, Benvolio's horns again!

MARTINO. O, misery!—How now, Benvolio!

BENVOLIO. Defend me, heaven! shall I be haunted still?

MARTINO. Nay, fear not, man; we have no power to kill.

BENVOLIO. My friends transformed thus! O, hellish spite!
Your heads are all set with horns.

FREDERICK. You hit it right;
It is your own you mean; feel on your head.

BENVOLIO. Zounds, horns again!

MARTINO. Nay, chafe not, man; we all are sped.

BENVOLIO. What devil attends this damn'd magician,
That, spite of spite, our wrongs are doubled?

FREDERICK. What may we do, that we may hide our shames?

BENVOLIO. If we should follow him to work revenge,
He'd join long asses' ears to these huge horns,
And make us laughing-stocks to all the world.

MARTINO. What shall we, then, do, dear Benvolio?

BENVOLIO. I have a castle joining near these woods;
And thither we'll repair, and live obscure,
Till time shall alter these our brutish shapes:
Sith black disgrace hath thus eclips'd our fame,
We'll rather die with grief than live with shame.
    [Exeunt.]

Enter FAUSTUS, a HORSE-COURSER, and MEPHISTOPHILIS.

HORSE-COURSER. I beseech your worship, accept of these forty
dollars.

FAUSTUS. Friend, thou canst not buy so good a horse for so small
a price. I have no great need to sell him: but, if thou likest
him for ten dollars more, take him, because I see thou hast a
good mind to him.

HORSE-COURSER. I beseech you, sir, accept of this: I am a very poor man, and have lost very much of late by horse-flesh, and this bargain will set me up again.

FAUSTUS. Well, I will not stand with thee: give me the money [HORSE-COURSER gives FAUSTUS the money]. Now, sirrah, I must tell you that you may ride him o'er hedge and ditch, and spare him not; but, do you hear? in any case, ride him not into the water.

HORSE-COURSER. How, sir! not into the water! why, will he not drink of all waters?

FAUSTUS. Yes, he will drink of all waters; but ride him not into the water: o'er hedge and ditch, or where thou wilt, but not into the water. Go, bid the hostler deliver him unto you, and remember what I say.

HORSE-COURSER. I warrant you, sir!—O, joyful day! now am I a made man for ever.
    [Exit.]

FAUSTUS. What art thou, Faustus, but a man condemn'd to die?
Thy fatal time draws to a final end;
Despair doth drive distrust into my thoughts:
Confound these passions with a quiet sleep:
Tush, Christ did call the thief upon the Cross;
Then rest thee, Faustus, quiet in conceit.
    [He sits to sleep.]

    Re-enter the HORSE-COURSER, wet.

HORSE-COURSER. O, what a cozening doctor was this! I, riding my horse into the water, thinking some hidden mystery had been in the horse, I had nothing under me but a little straw, and had much ado to escape drowning. Well, I'll go rouse him, and make him give me my forty dollars again.—Ho, sirrah Doctor, you cozening scab! Master Doctor, awake, and rise, and give me my money again, for your horse is turned to a bottle of hay, Master Doctor! [He pulls off FAUSTUS' leg]. Alas, I am undone! what shall I do? I have pulled off his leg.

FAUSTUS. O, help, help! the villain hath murdered me.

HORSE-COURSER. Murder or not murder, now he has but one leg, I'll outrun him, and cast this leg into some ditch or other.
    [Aside, and then runs out.]

FAUSTUS. Stop him, stop him, stop him!—Ha, ha, ha! Faustus hath his leg again, and the Horse-courser a bundle of hay for his forty dollars.

    Enter WAGNER.

How now, Wagner! what news with thee?

WAGNER. If it please you, the Duke of Vanholt doth earnestly entreat your company, and hath sent some of his men to attend you, with provision fit for your journey.

FAUSTUS. The Duke of Vanholt's an honourable gentleman, and one to whom I must be no niggard of my cunning. Come, away!
    [Exeunt.

    Enter ROBIN, DICK, the HORSE-COURSER, and a CARTER.

CARTER. Come, my masters, I'll bring you to the best beer in Europe.—What, ho, hostess! where be these whores?

    Enter HOSTESS.

HOSTESS. How now! what lack you? What, my old guess! welcome.

ROBIN. Sirrah Dick, dost thou know why I stand so mute?

DICK. No, Robin: why is't?

ROBIN. I am eighteen-pence on the score. but say nothing; see if she have forgotten me.

HOSTESS. Who's this that stands so solemnly by himself? What, my old guest!

ROBIN. O, hostess, how do you? I hope my score stands still.

HOSTESS. Ay, there's no doubt of that; for methinks you make no haste to wipe it out.

DICK. Why, hostess, I say, fetch us some beer.

HOSTESS. You shall presently.—Look up into the hall there, ho!
  [Exit.—Drink is presently brought in.]

DICK. Come, sirs, what shall we do now till mine hostess comes?

CARTER. Marry, sir, I'll tell you the bravest tale how a
conjurer served me. You know Doctor Faustus?

HORSE-COURSER. Ay, a plague take him! here's some on's have cause
to know him. Did he conjure thee too?

CARTER. I'll tell you how he served me. As I was going to
Wittenberg, t'other day, with a load of hay, he met me, and
asked me what he should give me for as much hay as he could eat.
Now, sir, I thinking that a little would serve his turn, bad him
take as much as he would for three farthings: so he presently
gave me my money and fell to eating; and, as I am a cursen
man, he never left eating till he had eat up all my load of hay.

ALL. O, monstrous! eat a whole load of hay!

ROBIN. Yes, yes, that may be; for I have heard of one that has eat
a load of logs.

HORSE-COURSER. Now, sirs, you shall hear how villanously he
served me. I went to him yesterday to buy a horse of him, and
he would by no means sell him under forty dollars. So, sir,
because I knew him to be such a horse as would run over hedge
and ditch and never tire, I gave him his money. So, when I had
my horse, Doctor Faustus bad me ride him night and day, and spare
him no time; but, quoth he, in any case, ride him not into the
water. Now, sir, I thinking the horse had had some quality
that he would not have me know of, what did I but rid him
into a great river? and when I came just in the midst, my horse
vanished away, and I sate straddling upon a bottle of hay.

ALL. O, brave doctor!

HORSE-COURSER. But you shall hear how bravely I served him for it. I
went me home to his house, and there I found him asleep.

I kept a hallooing and whooping in his ears; but all could not wake him. I, seeing that, took him by the leg, and never rested pulling till I had pulled me his leg quite off; and now 'tis at home in mine hostry.

ROBIN. And has the doctor but one leg, then? that's excellent; for one of his devils turned me into the likeness of an ape's face.

CARTER. Some more drink, hostess!

ROBIN. Hark you, we'll into another room and drink a while, and then we'll go seek out the doctor.
[Exeunt.]

Enter the DUKE OF VANHOLT, his DUCHESS, FAUSTUS, MEPHISTOPHILIS, and ATTENDANTS.

DUKE. Thanks, Master Doctor, for these pleasant sights; nor know I how sufficiently to recompense your great deserts in erecting that enchanted castle in the air, the sight whereof so delighted me as nothing in the world could please me more.

FAUSTUS. I do think myself, my good lord, highly recompensed in that it pleaseth your grace to think but well of that which Faustus hath performed.—But, gracious lady, it may be that you have taken no pleasure in those sights; therefore, I pray you tell me, what is the thing you most desire to have; be it in the world, it shall be yours: I have heard that great-bellied women do long for things are rare and dainty.

DUCHESS. True, Master Doctor; and, since I find you so kind, I will make known unto you what my heart desires to have; and, were it now summer, as it is January, a dead time of the winter, I would request no better meat than a dish of ripe grapes.

FAUSTUS. This is but a small matter.—Go, Mephistophilis; away!
[Exit MEPHISTOPHILIS.]
Madam, I will do more than this for your content.

Re-Enter MEPHISTOPHILIS with grapes.

Here now, taste you these: they should be good, for they come from a far country, I can tell you.

DUKE. This makes me wonder more than all the rest, that at this time of the year, when every tree is barren of his fruit, from whence you had these ripe grapes.

FAUSTUS. Please it your grace, the year is divided into two circles over the whole world; so that, when it is winter with us, in the contrary circle it is likewise summer with them, as in India, Saba, and such countries that lie far east, where they have fruit twice a-year; from whence, by means of a swift spirit that I have, I had these grapes brought, as you see.

DUCHESS. And, trust me, they are the sweetest grapes that e'er I tasted.

The CLOWNS bounce at the gate, within.

DUKE. What rude disturbers have we at the gate?
Go, pacify their fury, set it ope,
And then demand of them what they would have.

[They knock again, and call out to talk with FAUSTUS.]

SERVANT. Why, how now, masters! what a coil is there!
What is the reason you disturb the Duke?

DICK [within]. We have no reason for it; therefore a fig for him!

SERVANT. Why, saucy varlets, dare you be so bold?

HORSE-COURSER [within]. I hope, sir, we have wit enough to be more bold than welcome.

SERVANT. It appears so: pray, be bold elsewhere, and trouble not the Duke.

DUKE. What would they have?

SERVANT. They all cry out to speak with Doctor Faustus.

CARTER [within]. Ay, and we will speak with him.

DUKE. Will you, sir?—Commit the rascals.

DICK [within]. Commit with us! he were as good commit with his
father as commit with us.

FAUSTUS. I do beseech your grace, let them come in;
They are good subject for a merriment.

DUKE. Do as thou wilt, Faustus; I give thee leave.

FAUSTUS. I thank your grace.

Enter ROBIN, DICK, CARTER, and HORSE-COURSER.

Why, how now, my good friends!
Faith, you are too outrageous: but, come near;
I have procur'd your pardons: welcome, all.

ROBIN. Nay, sir, we will be welcome for our money, and we will
pay for what we take.—What, ho! give's half a dozen of beer here,
and be hanged!

FAUSTUS. Nay, hark you; can you tell me where you are?

CARTER. Ay, marry, can I; we are under heaven.

SERVANT. Ay; but, Sir Saucebox, know you in what place?

HORSE-COURSER. Ay, ay, the house is good enough to drink in.
—Zouns, fill us some beer, or we'll break all the barrels in
the house, and dash out all your brains with your bottles!

FAUSTUS. Be not so furious: come, you shall have beer.—
My lord, beseech you give me leave a while;
I'll gage my credit 'twill content your grace.

DUKE. With all my heart, kind doctor; please thyself;
Our servants and our court's at thy command.

FAUSTUS. I humbly thank your grace.—Then fetch some beer.

HORSE-COURSER. Ay, marry, there spake a doctor, indeed!
and, faith, I'll drink a health to thy wooden leg for that word.

FAUSTUS. My wooden leg! what dost thou mean by that?

CARTER. Ha, ha, ha!—Dost hear him, Dick? he has forgot his leg.

HORSE-COURSER. Ay, ay, he does not stand much upon that.

FAUSTUS. No, faith; not much upon a wooden leg.

CARTER. Good Lord, that flesh and blood should be so frail with your worship! Do not you remember a horse-courser you sold a horse to?

FAUSTUS. Yes, I remember I sold one a horse.

CARTER. And do you remember you bid he should not ride him into the water?

FAUSTUS. Yes, I do very well remember that.

CARTER. And do you remember nothing of your leg?

FAUSTUS. No, in good sooth.

CARTER. Then, I pray you, remember your courtesy.

FAUSTUS. I thank you, sir.

CARTER. 'Tis not so much worth. I pray you, tell me one thing.

FAUSTUS. What's that?

CARTER. Be both your legs bed-fellows every night together?

FAUSTUS. Wouldst thou make a Colossus of me, that thou askest me such questions?

CARTER. No, truly, sir; I would make nothing of you; but I would fain know that.

    Enter HOSTESS with drink.
FAUSTUS. Then, I assure thee certainly, they are.

CARTER. I thank you; I am fully satisfied.

FAUSTUS. But wherefore dost thou ask?

CARTER. For nothing, sir: but methinks you should have a wooden bed-fellow of one of 'em.

HORSE-COURSER. Why, do you hear, sir? did not I pull off one of your legs when you were asleep?

FAUSTUS. But I have it again, now I am awake: look you here, sir.

ALL. O, horrible! had the doctor three legs?

CARTER. Do you remember, sir, how you cozened me, and eat up my load of——

[FAUSTUS, in the middle of each speech, charms them dumb.]

DICK. Do you remember how you made me wear an ape's——

HORSE-COURSER. You whoreson conjuring scab, do you remember how you cozened me with a ho——

ROBIN. Ha' you forgotten me? you think to carry it away with your hey-pass and re-pass: do you remember the dog's fa——
    [Exeunt CLOWNS.]

HOSTESS. Who pays for the ale? hear you, Master Doctor; now you have sent away my guess, I pray who shall pay me for my a——
    [Exit HOSTESS.]

DUCHESS. My lord,
We are much beholding to this learned man.

DUKE. So are we, madam; which we will recompense
With all the love and kindness that we may:
His artful sport drives all sad thoughts away.
    [Exeunt.]

    Thunder and lightning. Enter DEVILS with covered dishes;
        MEPHISTOPHILIS leads them into FAUSTUS'S study; then enter
        WAGNER.

WAGNER. I think my master means to die shortly; he has made
his will, and given me his wealth, his house, his goods, and
store of golden plate, besides two thousand ducats ready-coined.
I wonder what he means: if death were nigh, he would not frolic
thus. He's now at supper with the scholars, where there's such
belly-cheer as Wagner in his life ne'er saw the like: and,
see where they come! belike the feast is ended.
    [Exit.]

    Enter FAUSTUS, MEPHISTOPHILIS, and two or three SCHOLARS.

FIRST SCHOLAR. Master Doctor Faustus, since our conference
about fair ladies, which was the beautifulest in all the world,
we have determined with ourselves that Helen of Greece was the
admirablest lady that ever lived: therefore, Master Doctor, if
you will do us so much favour as to let us see that peerless
dame of Greece, whom all the world admires for majesty, we should
think ourselves much beholding unto you.

FAUSTUS. Gentlemen,
For that I know your friendship is unfeign'd,
It is not Faustus' custom to deny
The just request of those that wish him well:
You shall behold that peerless dame of Greece,
No otherwise for pomp or majesty
Than when Sir Paris cross'd the seas with her,
And brought the spoils to rich Dardania.
Be silent, then, for danger is in words.

    Music sounds. MEPHISTOPHILIS brings in HELEN; she passeth
over the stage.

SECOND SCHOLAR. Was this fair Helen, whose admired worth
Made Greece with ten years' war afflict poor Troy?

THIRD SCHOLAR. Too simple is my wit to tell her worth,
Whom all the world admires for majesty.

FIRST SCHOLAR. Now we have seen the pride of Nature's work,
We'll take our leaves: and, for this blessed sight,
Happy and blest be Faustus evermore!

FAUSTUS. Gentlemen, farewell: the same wish I to you.
   [Exeunt SCHOLARS.]

   Enter an OLD MAN.

OLD MAN. O gentle Faustus, leave this damned art,
This magic, that will charm thy soul to hell,
And quite bereave thee of salvation!
Though thou hast now offended like a man,
Do not persever in it like a devil:
Yet, yet thou hast an amiable soul,
If sin by custom grow not into nature;
Then, Faustus, will repentance come too late;
Then thou art banish'd from the sight of heaven:
No mortal can express the pains of hell.
It may be, this my exhortation
Seems harsh and all unpleasant: let it not;
For, gentle son, I speak it not in wrath,
Or envy of thee, but in tender love,
And pity of thy future misery;
And so have hope that this my kind rebuke,
Checking thy body, may amend thy soul.

FAUSTUS. Where art thou, Faustus? wretch, what hast thou done?
Hell claims his right, and with a roaring voice
Says, "Faustus, come; thine hour is almost come;"
And Faustus now will come to do thee right.

   [MEPHISTOPHILIS gives him a dagger.]

OLD MAN. O, stay, good Faustus, stay thy desperate steps!
I see an angel hover o'er thy head,
And, with a vial full of precious grace,
Offers to pour the same into thy soul:
Then call for mercy, and avoid despair.

FAUSTUS. O friend, I feel
Thy words to comfort my distressed soul!
Leave me a while to ponder on my sins.

OLD MAN. Faustus, I leave thee; but with grief of heart,
Fearing the enemy of thy hapless soul.
   [Exit.]

FAUSTUS. Accursed Faustus, wretch, what hast thou done?
I do repent; and yet I do despair:
Hell strives with grace for conquest in my breast:
What shall I do to shun the snares of death?

MEPHIST. Thou traitor, Faustus, I arrest thy soul
For disobedience to my sovereign lord:
Revolt, or I'll in piece-meal tear thy flesh.

FAUSTUS. I do repent I e'er offended him.
Sweet Mephistophilis, entreat thy lord
To pardon my unjust presumption,
And with my blood again I will confirm
The former vow I made to Lucifer.

MEPHIST. Do it, then, Faustus, with unfeigned heart,
Lest greater dangers do attend thy drift.

FAUSTUS. Torment, sweet friend, that base and aged man,
That durst dissuade me from thy Lucifer,
With greatest torments that our hell affords.

MEPHIST. His faith is great; I cannot touch his soul;
But what I may afflict his body with
I will attempt, which is but little worth.

FAUSTUS. One thing, good servant, let me crave of thee,
To glut the longing of my heart's desire,—
That I may have unto my paramour
That heavenly Helen which I saw of late,
Whose sweet embraces may extinguish clean
Those thoughts that do dissuade me from my vow,
And keep my oath I made to Lucifer.

MEPHIST. This, or what else my Faustus shall desire,
Shall be perform'd in twinkling of an eye.

    Re-enter HELEN, passing over the stage between two CUPIDS.

FAUSTUS. Was this the face that launch'd a thousand ships,
And burnt the topless towers of Ilium?—
Sweet Helen, make me immortal with a kiss.—

[Kisses her.]
Her lips suck forth my soul: see, where it flies!—
Come, Helen, come, give me my soul again.
Here will I dwell, for heaven is in these lips,
And all is dross that is not Helena.
I will be Paris, and for love of thee,
Instead of Troy, shall Wittenberg be sack'd;
And I will combat with weak Menelaus,
And wear thy colours on my plumed crest;
Yea, I will wound Achilles in the heel,
And then return to Helen for a kiss.
O, thou art fairer than the evening air
Clad in the beauty of a thousand stars;
Brighter art thou than flaming Jupiter
When he appear'd to hapless Semele;
More lovely than the monarch of the sky
In wanton Arethusa's azur'd arms;
And none but thou shalt be my paramour!
[Exeunt.]

Thunder. Enter LUCIFER, BELZEBUB, and MEPHISTOPHILIS.

LUCIFER. Thus from infernal Dis do we ascend
To view the subjects of our monarchy,
Those souls which sin seals the black sons of hell;
'Mong which, as chief, Faustus, we come to thee,
Bringing with us lasting damnation
To wait upon thy soul: the time is come
Which makes it forfeit.

MEPHIST. And, this gloomy night,
Here, in this room, will wretched Faustus be.

BELZEBUB. And here we'll stay,
To mark him how he doth demean himself.

MEPHIST. How should he but in desperate lunacy?
Fond worldling, now his heart-blood dries with grief;
His conscience kills it; and his labouring brain
Begets a world of idle fantasies
To over-reach the devil; but all in vain;
His store of pleasures must be sauc'd with pain.
He and his servant Wagner are at hand;

Both come from drawing Faustus' latest will.
See, where they come!

Enter FAUSTUS and WAGNER.

FAUSTUS. Say, Wagner,—thou hast perus'd my will,—
How dost thou like it?

WAGNER. Sir, So wondrous well,
As in all humble duty I do yield
My life and lasting service for your love.

FAUSTUS. Gramercy, Wagner.

Enter SCHOLARS.

Welcome, Gentlemen.
    [Exit WAGNER.]

FIRST SCHOLAR. Now, worthy Faustus, methinks your looks are
chang'd.

FAUSTUS. O, gentlemen!

SECOND SCHOLAR. What ails Faustus?

FAUSTUS. Ah, my sweet chamber-fellow, had I lived with thee,
then had I lived still! but now must die eternally. Look, sirs,
comes he not? comes he not?

FIRST SCHOLAR. O my dear Faustus, what imports this fear?

SECOND SCHOLAR. Is all our pleasure turn'd to melancholy?

THIRD SCHOLAR. He is not well with being over-solitary.

SECOND SCHOLAR. If it be so, we'll have physicians,
And Faustus shall be cur'd.

THIRD SCHOLAR. 'Tis but a surfeit, sir; fear nothing.

FAUSTUS. A surfeit of deadly sin, that hath damned both
body and soul.

SECOND SCHOLAR. Yet, Faustus, look up to heaven, and remember mercy is infinite.

FAUSTUS. But Faustus' offence can ne'er be pardoned: the serpent that tempted Eve may be saved, but not Faustus. O gentlemen, hear me with patience, and tremble not at my speeches! Though my heart pant and quiver to remember that I have been a student here these thirty years, O, would I had never seen Wittenberg, never read book! and what wonders I have done, all Germany can witness, yea, all the world; for which Faustus hath lost both Germany and the world, yea, heaven itself, heaven, the seat of God, the throne of the blessed, the kingdom of joy; and must remain in hell for ever, hell. O, hell, for ever! Sweet friends, what shall become of Faustus, being in hell for ever?

SECOND SCHOLAR. Yet, Faustus, call on God.

FAUSTUS. On God, whom Faustus hath abjured! on God, whom Faustus hath blasphemed! O my God, I would weep! but the devil draws in my tears. Gush forth blood, instead of tears! yea, life and soul! O, he stays my tongue! I would lift up my hands; but see, they hold 'em, they hold 'em?

ALL. Who, Faustus?

FAUSTUS. Why, Lucifer and Mephistophilis. O gentlemen, I gave them my soul for my cunning!

ALL. O, God forbid!

FAUSTUS. God forbade it, indeed; but Faustus hath done it: for the vain pleasure of four-and-twenty years hath Faustus lost eternal joy and felicity. I writ them a bill with mine own blood: the date is expired; this is the time, and he will fetch me.

FIRST SCHOLAR. Why did not Faustus tell us of this before, that divines might have prayed for thee?

FAUSTUS. Oft have I thought to have done so; but the devil threatened to tear me in pieces, if I named God, to fetch me body and soul, if I once gave ear to divinity: and now 'tis too late. Gentlemen, away, lest you perish with me.

SECOND SCHOLAR. O, what may we do to save Faustus?

FAUSTUS. Talk not of me, but save yourselves, and depart.

THIRD SCHOLAR. God will strengthen me; I will stay with Faustus.

FIRST SCHOLAR. Tempt not God, sweet friend; but let us into the next
room, and pray for him.

FAUSTUS. Ay, pray for me, pray for me; and what noise soever
you hear, come not unto me, for nothing can rescue me.

SECOND SCHOLAR. Pray thou, and we will pray that God may have
mercy upon thee.

FAUSTUS. Gentlemen, farewell: if I live till morning, I'll visit
you; if not, Faustus is gone to hell.

ALL. Faustus, farewell.
   [Exeunt SCHOLARS.]

MEPHIST. Ay, Faustus, now thou hast no hope of heaven;
Therefore despair; think only upon hell,
For that must be thy mansion, there to dwell.

FAUSTUS. O thou bewitching fiend, 'twas thy temptation
Hath robb'd me of eternal happiness!

MEPHIST. I do confess it, Faustus, and rejoice:
'Twas I that, when thou wert i'the way to heaven,
Damm'd up thy passage; when thou took'st the book
To view the Scriptures, then I turn'd the leaves,
And led thine eye.
What, weep'st thou? 'tis too late; despair! Farewell:
Fools that will laugh on earth must weep in hell.
   [Exit.]

Enter GOOD ANGEL and EVIL ANGEL at several doors.

GOOD ANGEL. O Faustus, if thou hadst given ear to me,
Innumerable joys had follow'd thee!
But thou didst love the world.

EVIL ANGEL. Gave ear to me,
And now must taste hell-pains perpetually.

GOOD ANGEL. O, what will all thy riches, pleasures, pomps,
Avail thee now?

EVIL ANGEL. Nothing, but vex thee more,
To want in hell, that had on earth such store.

GOOD ANGEL. O, thou hast lost celestial happiness,
Pleasures unspeakable, bliss without end
Hadst thou affected sweet divinity,
Hell or the devil had had no power on thee:
Hadst thou kept on that way, Faustus, behold,
    [Music, while a throne descends.]
In what resplendent glory thou hadst sit
In yonder throne, like those bright-shining saints,
And triumph'd over hell! That hast thou lost;
And now, poor soul, must thy good angel leave thee:
The jaws of hell are open to receive thee.
    [Exit. The throne ascends.]

EVIL ANGEL. Now, Faustus, let thine eyes with horror stare
    [Hell is discovered.]
Into that vast perpetual torture-house:
There are the Furies tossing damned souls
On burning forks; there bodies boil in lead;
There are live quarters broiling on the coals,
That ne'er can die; this ever-burning chair
Is for o'er-tortur'd souls to rest them in;
These that are fed with sops of flaming fire,
Were gluttons, and lov'd only delicates,
And laugh'd to see the poor starve at their gates:
But yet all these are nothing; thou shalt see
Ten thousand tortures that more horrid be.

FAUSTUS. O, I have seen enough to torture me!

EVIL ANGEL. Nay, thou must feel them, taste the smart of all:
He that loves pleasure must for pleasure fall:
And so I leave thee, Faustus, till anon;
Then wilt thou tumble in confusion.
    [Exit. Hell disappears.—The clock strikes eleven.]

FAUSTUS. O Faustus,
Now hast thou but one bare hour to live,
And then thou must be damn'd perpetually!
Stand still, you ever-moving spheres of heaven,
That time may cease, and midnight never come;
Fair Nature's eye, rise, rise again, and make
Perpetual day; or let this hour be but
A year, a month, a week, a natural day,
That Faustus may repent and save his soul!
O lente, lente currite, noctis equi!
The stars move still, time runs, the clock will strike,
The devil will come, and Faustus must be damn'd.
O, I'll leap up to heaven!—Who pulls me down?—
See, where Christ's blood streams in the firmament!
One drop of blood will save me: O my Christ!—
Rend not my heart for naming of my Christ;
Yet will I call on him: O, spare me, Lucifer!—
Where is it now? 'tis gone:
And, see, a threatening arm, an angry brow!
Mountains and hills, come, come, and fall on me,
And hide me from the heavy wrath of heaven!
No!
Then will I headlong run into the earth:
Gape, earth! O, no, it will not harbour me!
You stars that reign'd at my nativity,
Whose influence hath allotted death and hell,
Now draw up Faustus, like a foggy mist,
Into the entrails of yon labouring clouds,
That, when you vomit forth into the air,
My limbs may issue from your smoky mouths;
But let my soul mount and ascend to heaven!
    [The clock strikes the half-hour.]
O, half the hour is past! 'twill all be past anon.
O, if my soul must suffer for my sin,
Impose some end to my incessant pain;
Let Faustus live in hell a thousand years,
A hundred thousand, and at last be sav'd!
No end is limited to damned souls.
Why wert thou not a creature wanting soul?
Or why is this immortal that thou hast?
O, Pythagoras' metempsychosis, were that true,
This soul should fly from me, and I be chang'd

68

Into some brutish beast! all beasts are happy,
For, when they die,
Their souls are soon dissolv'd in elements;
But mine must live still to be plagu'd in hell.
Curs'd be the parents that engender'd me!
No, Faustus, curse thyself, curse Lucifer
That hath depriv'd thee of the joys of heaven.
    [The clock strikes twelve.]
It strikes, it strikes! Now, body, turn to air,
Or Lucifer will bear thee quick to hell!
O soul, be chang'd into small water-drops,
And fall into the ocean, ne'er be found!

    Thunder. Enter DEVILS.

O, mercy, heaven! look not so fierce on me!
Adders and serpents, let me breathe a while!
Ugly hell, gape not! come not, Lucifer!
I'll burn my books!—O Mephistophilis!
    [Exeunt DEVILS with FAUSTUS.]

    Enter SCHOLARS.

FIRST SCHOLAR. Come, gentlemen, let us go visit Faustus,
For such a dreadful night was never seen;
Since first the world's creation did begin,
Such fearful shrieks and cries were never heard:
Pray heaven the doctor have escap'd the danger.

SECOND SCHOLAR.
O, help us, heaven! see, here are Faustus' limbs,
All torn asunder by the hand of death!

THIRD SCHOLAR.
The devils whom Faustus serv'd have torn him thus;
For, twixt the hours of twelve and one, methought,
I heard him shriek and call aloud for help;
At which self time the house seem'd all on fire
With dreadful horror of these damned fiends.

SECOND SCHOLAR. Well, gentlemen, though Faustus' end be such
As every Christian heart laments to think on,
Yet, for he was a scholar once admir'd

For wondrous knowledge in our German schools,
We'll give his mangled limbs due burial;
And all the students, cloth'd in mourning black,
Shall wait upon his heavy funeral.
    [Exeunt.]

Enter CHORUS.

CHORUS. Cut is the branch that might have grown full straight,
And burned is Apollo's laurel-bough,
That sometime grew within this learned man.
Faustus is gone: regard his hellish fall,
Whose fiendful fortune may exhort the wise,
Only to wonder at unlawful things,
Whose deepness doth entice such forward wits
To practise more than heavenly power permits.
    [Exit.]

Terminat hora diem; terminat auctor opus.

Printed in Great Britain
by Amazon